SAGEBRUSH REVIEW

TRANSGRESSION
&
PERSONA

XIII & XIV | SPRING 2019

Copyright © 2019 by *Sagebrush Review*.
All rights reserved.

ISBN: 978-0-9823453-9-9
Printed in the United States.

Sagebrush Review is a 501(c)(3) student-run, annual journal of literature, art, and photography published by the students of The University of Texas at San Antonio. *Sagebrush* also facilitates literary and art events at UTSA and throughout the city of San Antonio.

The University of Texas at San Antonio assumes no responsibility for the contents of this publication. The opinions expressed herein are not necessarily those of The University of Texas System, UTSA, or of UTSA's faculty, staff or students.

For more information about *Sagebrush Review* submissions, events, and internship openings, please email sagebrushreview@gmail.com, or visit www.sagebrushreview.org.

MANAGING EDITOR

Rachel Rivero
B.A. English, Concentration in Creative Writing

EDITORS

Dorielys Cruz
*B.A. English, Concentration in Creative Writing,
Minor in Anthropology*

Sabrina Longoria
*B.A. English, Concentration in Creative Writing,
Certificate in Professional Writing*

Maxwell Meier
B.A. English, Concentration in Creative Writing

Lori Hunt
B.A. English, Concentration in Creative Writing

The Staff of *Sagebrush Review* would like to thank everyone who aided in the publication of the combined 2018 and 2019 issue, including our Faculty Advisor, Dr. David Ray Vance for his experitse and guidance, Dr. Wendy Barker (Pearl LeWinn Endowmed Chair of Creative Writing) for her kindness and generous donations, The Department of English at UTSA for allowing us to work within their office, and everyone who submitted their exceptional pieces to both issues. While we couldn't accept every single one, we feel that the ones in this combined issue represent the individuality and creativity that we strive towards in the pursuit and appreciation of the arts.

We sincerely hope you enjoy reading this issue as much as we did putting it together.

CONTENTS

EDITORS' CHOICE AWARDS

The Staff of Sagebrush Review would like to highlight the selected pieces for best in category for the combined 2018 & 2019 issue.

ART

Katherine Hatfield Cisneros
Pixels (front cover)

Michael Butkovich
Lay Me Down...Goodbye (back cover)

POETRY

Emily Turner
Clinging 11

Elyse Guziewicz
Sepulchre 12

PROSE

Mialise Carney
His Name Was Skylark 14

Ronald Philip Williams
Thunder 22

Xiomara Alejandro Martinez
En La Vida Hay Que Crecer   24
Mourning   26
White Flags   28

Michael Butkovich
A Mid-Summer's Childhood Horror Memory   30
A Moist Wet Morning   33
Cate's Eyes   35
Gypsy Stare   36
Stoic Lips   37

Joaquin Castillo
Altar   38

Jamie Crosswhite
Lived In   40

Dorielys Cruz
Monsters   42

Alexandra Daggett
Oceans   43

Loverra Di Giustino
Beetle   45
Drowning Late Night Cues   47
Holy Caucasian   48
Mother   50
Mouth Hyper   52
Run Queen   54

Chelsea Nguyen
Blunt Blade   56

Teja Dusanapudi
A Jumble of Rocks and Stones In Your Throat   58

Elyse Guziewicz
    Litany   60

Mary Halfmann
    A Lump in Her Oatmeal   61
    Gaslighting: A Catechism of Egg Shells   63
    The Girl they Called Skelator in Lakehills, Texas   65

Karen Hatfield Cisneros
    Posed   67

Nicholas Kelley
    And If You Ask Ganymede?   68

Emerson Little
    Changes   69
    Jailed Hopes   70

Raquel Lopez
    Yellow Bliss   71

Osamah Mandawi
    After the Ship Went Down   72
    Memories in Overhead Bins   73
    Observational Study of One Tree's Excessive Extrovert Behavior   74
    Rotten Relic from 2018   76

Aaron Martinez
    In a Dive Bar at the End of the World   77
    (Trans)sexual   78

M. C. Maxwell
    A Poet's Death   79
    A Poet's Passion   81

Emil Meila
   After Auerbach   83
   Girl Ghost   84
   How I Cured My Trichotillomania   85
   Self In Sea   86
   Self Portrait With Yellow Roses   87
   Shh…You've Been Preparing For This All Your Life   88

Dexter Morales
   1942   89

Gabriella Pawelek
   Old Customs / Over the Ouija Board   91

Kelci Piavis
   Allen Ginsberg   93

Victoria Ramirez Gentry
   Always After   95
   Wake   96

Xavier Reyna
   God Is...   98
   Poem For My Fathers   99
   Sueños De Verano   100
   Untitled 13   101

Brianna Schunk
   Lateral Knots   102
   My Body is Not a Flower   103
   Spotlight   104

Morgan Spalding
   Whore   106

Lemuel Torres
   Untitled I   109

Krystal Trlicek
I Can Remember — 110
Seventy-One Percent — 112

Emily Turner
Interplace Rd. — 114
Sun & Stars — 116

Matthew Vernon
Witness — 118

Quintin Walton
Prostitution Town — 120

Ronald Philip Williams
Devil's Wear — 122
Fallen — 123
Lauren's Interlude — 124
Your Heart is Beating — 126

Anjelica Zapata
Dirty Thoughts: Better To Be Left Unheard, Unread — 127

Vanessa Zimmerman
Taste Aversion — 129

EDITORS' CHOICE AWARD
FOR POETRY

Emily Turner

CLINGING

We were rose petal promises,
    Hand-washed wine glass glances.
We were early autumn leaf lust,
    Highway cigarette ash arrogance.
We were damp newspaper negligence,
    Worn-out rainboot souls.
We were things reduced to almost nothing,
    Clinging relentlessly to the in between.
We were too-soon I-love-you's,
    Two halves that never wholed.

EDITORS' CHOICE AWARD
FOR POETRY

Elyse Guziewicz

SEPULCHRE

    she's born blonde, but when
    she's three weeks old her hair
    falls out, grows back in dark.

    maybe it was the other way
    around—a brunette infant
    baptized and christened, water burning
    her baby skin, hair growing
    back blonde as eve before the serpent
    coiled around her leg, promised
    knowledge over ignorance.

    she's four when she says the words.
    six. nine. ten. at eleven,
    she loves a boy. her best friend
    told her so, and she'd believe
    anything hanging off that glossy mouth,
    wondering what flavor lip smackers she wears,
    how it would taste on her tongue.

    she's five-foot-five. six. seven.
    her skirts are three two one
    inches below the knee three two
    one inch above the collarbone three
    two-one poems for the girl she loves
    tucked away in her bra, in the drafts
    of her texts, in her pillowcase, in
    the sides of her bible with the
    bulletins and cantata programs bearing

her name. she holds them to her breast, to
cover herself, the easy way bony hands skittered
across her neck, tugging at her collar
leaving marks that burn and choke under the
piercing scrutiny of sunday mornings
the tired sermons of sunday night, the
gossip-fueled piety of prayer dripping from her tongue:

                              on her knees at altar call,
                                  begging for forgiveness.
                            on her knees in the soft dark
                 pressing kisses into her lover's hipbones,
                              making need for it again.

EDITORS' CHOICE AWARD
FOR PROSE

Mialise Carney

HIS NAME WAS SKYLARK

His name was Skylark. In his spare time, he liked to listen to music in languages he couldn't understand, watch old classic movies he didn't like, and think about people he'd never talk to. His name was Skylark, and he was terrified of birds.

Everything about birds scared Skylark. He didn't like their extendable necks, or their spear-like beaks, or their unblinking marbled eyes. He especially didn't enjoy their ability to make home in places he couldn't reach. Birds tamed a place he could not see or have, and that scared him.

It took Skylark a long time to realize it was the birds that were the enemies and not the people. When Skylark was young, he was not terrified of birds, instead most people in general. Although he would not hide or run screaming away from them like he did now with birds, he would stand quietly beside his mother, watching and waiting for a sign of their immanent attack. Skylark grew up thinking that the people were the ones draining his brain, but he now understood it was the birds pecking into his soft gray matter.

Skylark gained this new perspective not long after watching Alfred Hitchcock's *The Birds*, and despite how much his conscience told him that he was merely picking it up from the critically acclaimed horror movie, his logic told him that the birds truly had always been the ones eating him from the inside out.

Skylark was like every good son. He never told his mother about his constant vigilance towards the birds. In third grade, they found him screaming in the boy's bathroom with his head in the shallow corner of the wall. He was screaming that the people were trying to steal his ears for then he hadn't quite realized it was in fact the birds, not the people. They sent him home early with a peppermint, his mother acquitting his hysterics to a fever he came down with not long after the incident. Besides a few other public accidents, Skylark was content with merely keeping his suffering silent.

Skylark had a best friend. His name was Noah. Noah was a year older, but was in the same grade because when he was five his mother had been too drunk to remember to enroll him in the first grade. The state claims that they keep track of those things, but clearly, Noah was an example of what George Double-U-Bush called "Falling Through the Cracks." Even in later years, Noah was a child often left behind.

Noah and Skylark got along well, mostly because Noah thought and said strange things sometimes too. This was mostly because Noah was always high. Sometimes Skylark thought maybe he was high all of the time too because Noah only said strange things when he was high, and Skylark thought and said strange things even when he wasn't. Skylark liked Noah because Noah never told Skylark he was strange; they were both strange, and they were both okay with it.

Noah used to claim that he was Noah from Noah's Ark. He thought that Skylark was the bird that brought back the olive branch to show the prophet that the world was renewed and they could go back to ruining it. Despite the fact that Skylark knew the bird who brought back the olive branch was a dove, and not a skylark, he went along with it anyways. Noah was his best friend, and sometimes friends go along with lies in order to avoid becoming not best friends.

Now, Skylark would have to correct Noah despite not wanting to. Skylark could not be compared to or be seen as working alongside the creatures that tormented him. His rotting brain was being pulled apart like carrion; he simply could not allow Noah to see him as one of Them.

After they found Noah hanging from a belt in the basement, Skylark realized that he couldn't warn anybody or trust anybody with the knowledge of the birds. The birds were always listening, the birds could always hear. Skylark could not risk angering them, so he would have to work around them.

After the birds got Noah, Skylark started going to the public pool after school. After Noah, Skylark learned that being alive was easier alone, and so he would go to the pool and hold his breath underwater. He didn't have real swim trunks, so he would jump in with just his long underwear. He thought that the weird looks he got were because of his old Spongebob underwear, but it was probably because it appeared as if he was trying to drown himself. Skylark would ball himself up and hold his breath so long that the pimply 16-year-old life guard would jump in and drag him out.

Skylark felt like a slab of bacon sizzling on that dark stucco-concrete, his wet back burning as the life guard tried to get him to breathe. Skylark never inhaled water, but after Noah his body just stopped wanting air.

Skylark liked to be under the water because he felt that the birds could not get to him there. He wouldn't open his eye and he would stay frozen, allowing his body to be moved only by the splashing and the bumping of other people, the unaware and unprotected. Sometimes someone would kick him, or dive down and poke at him, but otherwise, he was perfectly alone at the bottom of the deep end. It was a good run for Skylark, until he realized that penguins were birds and they were excellent swimmers. After that, he stopped going to the pool.

Despite the fact that Skylark was alone by default, he liked being alone. Most people are alone because they are unbearable, a jerk, or shy—which sometimes are considered all the same thing—and they don't like being an anomaly. They reach out in any way that they can, but Skylark did everything to the best of his ability to stay out of the grasp of the wandering hands. Maybe it was the result of the majority of his childhood being distrustful of the people, or maybe he just liked the loneliness. Either way, he avoided people by eating lunch crouched on the toilets in the schools most disused bathrooms, staying as close to the center of crowds as possible, and by spending most of his spare time in the basement with the lights off. Skylark was not an unreachable person; he was just the song on the radio that everyone claimed to have heard before, but couldn't quite place who sang it, or where it came from.

But Skylark didn't mind any of this. Before, he thought it was the people that were trying to take him, and that is why he avoided them. Now that he knew the people were not the enemy, he knew that it was his job to protect them. Skylark's perspective was easily shifted, and after Noah was thwarted by the evil little creatures, Skylark felt a superman-like need to be a watchful guardian. He was terrified of the birds, but in a way, the birds gave him purpose.

Skylark did a lot of watching. That's what lonely people do. They watch, and they process, and they learn. Every tic and eye roll, every uncomfortable shift of weight onto a new leg, Skylark watched, and learned. Skylark watched the people, then Skylark watched the birds. Skylark watched the people again, to see if there were signs of when the birds would claim the people next.

After Noah, Skylark began to wonder if there could be a pattern. In his mind, random killings were less likely than systematic premeditated ones, so the only logical chance was that another bird-related murder was to happen soon. Despite his fear, Skylark knew that he would need to go on-site; he could no longer just watch and wait.

Finding patterns was undeniably difficult. Skylark did not know where to look, so he decided to start remembering the weird and unusual behaviors that Noah had expressed before the birds strung him up on the beam in his mother's basement. Noah had been a difficult person to read, for Skylark, because he was high too much and his behavior was always inconsistent. Going after the only lead he had, Skylark started to have lunch in the stoner bathroom instead of the bathroom next to the gym.

Her name was Minnie. He noticed her as he was crouched on the toilet in the stoner bathroom, with the stall door just slightly cracked. She was a year above Skylark and hung out with her boyfriend in the stoner bathroom. She smoked a lot and a little at the same time, because as Skylark watched her, he saw that she didn't inhale like she was supposed to. Not like Noah used to. Noah drank up the smoke like it was his last chance at breathing. Minnie sipped it like it was hot chocolate. Minnie did not seem like a victim.

Minnie had short hair. It bounced when she walked and it bounced when she laughed. Minnie always had scratches on her arms and hands. After school she would kiss her boyfriend on the cheek and ride her bike home, even in the rain. It was periwinkle and rusted, and her eyeliner would run down her face. She looked deflated and melted, like the Wicked Witch of the West.

They found Minnie two weeks later, slumped against a slide in the preschool playground. They said her boyfriend dealt her the lethal dose that had put her to sleep on that slide forever. They said she had scratches all over her face but Skylark didn't wait for an explanation because he knew it was the birds anyways. It turned out everyone could be a victim, even someone like Minnie.

Skylark went to the pool to think. The pimply 16-year-old lifeguard told him he was not allowed in to the pool without the proper flotation device, and he was not allowed past three feet. Skylark tried it, for a bit at first, but his body weight had become so small that he couldn't even force himself against the vest, bobbing his head into the water trying to reach the underwater silence he had come for. He realized he felt too much like a diving duck and quickly got out of the water, leaving the orange flotation device behind in the pool.

Skylark went down to the swing set where Minnie had been savagely murdered. The leaves on the trees were turning orange, the burnt kind. He climbed onto the swing set beside the slide where they found her. Skylark was having trouble trying to understand why Minnie was a victim. But somehow, he knew that someone would be next, and he would have to prevent it.

After Minnie, Skylark's brain became more rotted than before. This time he could feel his gray matter becoming stamped on, mushed and remolded into shapes he could not recognize. As he laid in bed at night, he could hear the sloshing and feel the sharp pricks of the bird's beaks ripping his pathways apart. Fear seized him, but then dissipated. The birds were remastering his brain one piece at a time, as his limbs became soft as spaghetti, he felt himself turning from a sprinting prey to a docile doe.

He realized connections became less clear. He ate his tuna fish sandwich squished into the stoner bathroom, trying to see if there was another victim he could spot. But the stoner bathroom was not the same without Minnie Schmitt; there was no atmosphere anymore. Students only came in quickly, they didn't talk like they used to. Skylark could not find the connection that he was looking for, so he stopped looking there.

Skylark was having trouble deciding where to next look, and he was also having trouble caring. He felt evaporated, tired, swelling. He would lay on his back for hours after school, with his eyes wide open without being able to see anything but the fuzzy blackness eating at the corners of his eyes. He didn't care, but he knew he had to.

The stoner connection clearly was not upholding so he began to look elsewhere. He looked for periwinkle rust, just like the bike Minnie used to fall apart on. It was surprisingly easy for Skylark to find who the next victim was.

Her name was Donna. It was not hard to find her, if anything it was hard to miss her. She always wore purple, and she had hair the color of rust. It was long and curly and listless. Donna was the center of attention, and Skylark bumped into her during a school assembly while he was hiding in the middle of the crowd. There had always been something different about her popularity, because when he bumped into her, she hadn't turned up her lip and flinched away, but instead glanced a freckled smile. Her name was Donna, and this time Skylark knew instantly that she was next.

Everyone loved Donna. Her prize was her hair, and her friends would stroke it in homeroom, twirling the ringlets around their sharp fingers. They looked like they wanted to rip it off but smiled and blinked sincerely when Donna would turn to look at them over her shoulder. Donna was the kind of pretty that made people hate her, and she knew it.

Skylark watched her during lunch, moving from the stoner bathroom to the picnic table outside on the lawn. She sat on the table with her group, throwing popcorn at each other. Donna did not seem like a victim, but this time, that security did not fool Skylark.

Three weeks after Skylark started watching Donna, Donna came to school with all of her hair cut off. All of her heavy curls, buzzed and buffed off to a short, blonde pixie cut that silenced the hallways as she moved through, dressed in an ugly green turtleneck. Skylark knew then he was right: Donna had been caught.

Before Christmas break, Donna held a Secret Santa. Skylark, of course, was not included, but Skylark still went just to see what presents were being given away. He sat in the corner on the bleachers, blissfully out of sight as he watched Donna break the rules of Secret Santa and give everyone a gift. Donna didn't give gift cards, or Lush lotions, or Yankee Candles. She gave away purple hair ties, and stuffed animals, and her favorite sweaters. It was obvious she was doomed.

Frozen on the bleachers, Skylark couldn't move. The initiative he felt after Noah was gone—the superhero sense of strength to Serve And Protect had evaporated just as fast the liquid that kept his brain afloat. He left the auditorium without looking back; later he'd blame his lapse in strength on the birds.

They found her December 26th in the bathtub. They said she did not leave a note, but that didn't throw Skylark; murder victims hardly leave comments. She left behind only "some birds are not meant to be caged" on her profile page, for all the world to see. A reason, or a warning. For Skylark, it was an answer.

Skylark spent winter vacation laying on his bedroom floor with the lights off. He couldn't even go to the pool this time; it had been drained months ago. His mother stood at the crack of his adjacent bedroom door, the yellow of the hall light illuminating her crossed arms and purple bathrobe.

It didn't take Skylark long to begin seeing the victim in his eyes when he looked in the mirror at night. It was then that he realized what all the murdered had in common, they all had eyes like the birds; glazed over, unseeing, marbled. It was something he never thought he would have become accustomed to, but as he stared at his own glazed over reflection, his eyes turned from gray to the black and beady. It was then that he knew he was next.

Skylark didn't panic at this realization like at the beginning he thought he would have. Like anyone would have expected him to. He didn't blink, in fact. Once prey is caught, it is hard to feel the desire to run.

Skylark did not run. Instead, Skylark flew. And he forgot what it felt like to be human, if there is any way to really feel human at all. He left his house in the middle of the night and went back to the playground where they found Minnie. Staring down from the oak tree he'd climbed, Skylark realized that sometimes you beat the birds, and sometimes you become them.

EDITORS' CHOICE AWARD
FOR PROSE

Ronald Philip Williams

THUNDER

Emilia. Ice down my veins, fire in my chest.

Her face had this tease to it that made you want to deflower her on sight. Her lips are as big as melons, and her tongue a peachy-pink that slithers through your mouth with ease. I could fuck her for a week and it wouldn't be enough. I could taste each inch of her lovely body and my taste-buds wouldn't be satisfied. Hungry.

She came over one night after one of my famous *red wine and write your bloody heart out* nights. She said I was fun to be around those nights. She said I got more witty and sexually charming than usual. And I must've been because her laughter lines had never been so distinct.

"Emilia, darling, you're quite the seducer coming over in your red-fitted dress with your hair all perfectly tangled like that. But I will not fall victim to your selfish libido. I will sit in this chair and finish this bottle and sleep the night away. You cannot stop me."

Emilia didn't speak. She did that often. When a challenge underestimated her power, she wouldn't speak. She'd act. Two long, sexy tan legs strutted towards me while the frame of her body swung with the music. *Frank Sinatra.*

"No no no no no, darling I know what you're doing but you must know, I am stronger than this."

Her legs hugged my back and her lips fought mine and my talking came to a halt. Kissing never felt so passionate to me. I've kissed plenty of women but none of them carried the raging hunger Emilia's kisses held. Our tongues felt like two swords in battle—striking to win, but deflected each time. I was too drunk to lose and she was too eager to win. Her hair-strands brushed the sides of my neck as her hand found the zipper to my black slacks.

Emilia. Ice down my veins, fire in my chest.

Xiomara Alejandro Martinez

EN LA VIDA HAY QUE CRECER

Poco a poco comenzamos a ver la luz.
Paso a paso crecemos sin comprenderlo,
Cambiando nuestras ilusiones por sueños nuevos,
Abriendo nuestros ojos a nuevos mundos.
Sonidos que no éramos capaces de oír, ahora nos arropan.
Nuestra alma ahora se agranda dentro de nuestro cuerpo.

No temas, mi cielo, por esos latidos que sientes
Ahora más fuerte que antes.
Es tu corazón, queriendo agarrar las nubes.
No dejes que el miedo te paralice, que te encierre en el pasado
Como un ruiseñor en cautiverio.
El miedo se alimenta de tus sueños y altera tu mente.
No lo persigas,
no lo llames,
no lo invites,
No lo enamores.

El corazón debe ser controlado a veces, es cierto.
Pero no aplastado, explotado y amargado
No debe ser obligado, frustrado o herido.
Cuídalo bien, será tu luz en el camino.

Cierra tus ojos una, dos, tres veces-hasta que te quede claro.
Que la vida no es para verla solamente.
Es para sentirla y saborearla, como vino del cielo.
Pues ya las nubes lo saben, las olas lo entienden, y lo practican.
Nosotros, los únicos, pasos atrás, atados al mundo,
sirviéndole al tiempo.

Poco a poco vamos aprendiendo a verlo diferente
Como lo hacen los niños, con esperanza.
Fíjate bien, y descubre tu vida otra vez.
Cántales a tus sueños, que lo oiga tu alma también.
No tengas miedo cariño, porque en la vida hay que crecer.

Xiomara Alejandro Martinez

MOURNING

                        Rustling leaves escaped the scene,
                        Along with a wishful wind wandering.
The icy vinyl pressed against my hand
Sending chills across my body
What kind of hell is this, that I stand here
                On a warm august day, the sunshine blaring
                The only arctic body in the room.
Staring at your face, the warmest it's ever been.
Oh, what cruel irony
You, smiling away at the sky,
        While I stand here, caressed only by my bitter tears.
If it were my wish, it would all be backward
The sun would not shine for months
                No faces disguised behind clown frowns
                Only you and I.
                But for once in my life I must learn to stay
                And you to leave.
Three gunshots fired for you into the air
Yet somehow, I feel them in my heart
Clashing, colliding, corroding
                  And thus, began
                  The cruelest sound of all
              The forced push of air
              Escaping my lungs sharply
The bitter huff of arctic,
Sterilized, metallic tint
The screeching of time as it edges on
Anciently.
                The scream of distance of
                Walls closing in.
            The orchestra of colors painting us

>   Seeping through into my
>   Very soul.
> Oh, never did I hate a sound as much
> As the one uttered,

>   ......The day the music died.

Xiomara Alejandro Martinez

WHITE FLAGS

    Thousands of white flags raised
    From thousands of breathless souls
    Who found no refuge in the eyes of a stranger.
    Whose only wish was for peace;
    End to this turmoil inside their heads
    Whose dreams disappeared into the merciless grave.
    By their own loving hands:
    One thousand hearts with no beat
    One thousand minds with no memories
    One thousand smiles melted
    Into white strips of fabric decorating the ground.
    In your endless sleep, my dear,
    I hope you don't dream
    Of the face with no kindness.
    I hope that face never looks like me.
    If only
    We'd been kind enough to carry our neighbor,
    Loving enough to be a friend.
    Bold enough to stand for the motionless
    Selfless enough to aid
    In the war inside your head.
    If only
    Someone had told you
    How important you were
    How missed you'd be
    Instead,
    We'd rather honor the dead
    Than fight for the living.
    In all this, I'll pray for
    One thing.

May God never allow me
To be the vacant stare you receive
When you were looking for a
Reason to live.

Michael Butkovich

A MID-SUMMER'S CHILDHOOD HORROR MEMORY

that tiny house which once held grandma's wonderful smells is no more
it only returns from time to time in faint limited fond touches of a garlicy memory
red chilies and green peppers soaked in olive oil, a fiesta blend that once was
Ben-gay on arms with homemade lily-weed ointment on legs, all topped off with Raid sprayed everywhere...

                                              are now no more

at five I was to find out just what it felt like to be broke-back
innocence stolen on a summers morning with cries that never did dry
who was I before that Domingo day ended who I was?
like the dead-end street that tiny house sat on, I too -ended there
who could have known a shared shower would change it all?

        mommy is who should have known, but lied in her own
        denial of it all

below a city street Kress café, I blabbed all
a slap to the face was all the truth awarded me
Catholic school like the Hippies of the times, taught me to tell it like it was
but mother's reality taught me differently
worse thing of all was the cutting of the strings...

                              mother no longer wore an apron for me

alone at five, alone still now
seeking always my stolen childhood summers memories
negativity drips upon my chin of bitter ill-gotten guidance they
forced fed me daily
while the Gordo Sundae was sprinkled with forgiveness
rebellious eating became my signal cry of despair…

                              but no one cared enough to notice

Frankenstein's house became my refuge
in the universal reality I found understanding on common graves of
fantasy
like the black and white creature that he was, rejected by his own
creator
I could relate, as my own womb-maker rejected me
Having not asked to be made then to be abandoned …

                              Both Frank and I never understood why?

now that tiny house is only a painful memory of the curse that follows me
from woman to woman, marriage to marriage my life's lost loves of
attempted mangled bonds
were all twisted loves of a twisted soul, seeking always absolution
through acceptance
like a broken toy a child cries over, never able to be truly replaced,
never forgetting the pain…

Michael Butkovich

                        this broken boy was equally ignored

No number of Griff's burgers and fries on long Corpus fishing trips, nor
Godzilla movie passes could never absolve the Sins of the past
Lennon's touch of Lucy with red golden smoked hairs of Mary, nor
refine nasal blizzard blasts never numbed the agony of living
Daydreaming of another life...

                    was all that was left, but even that was tainted
                    with negativity

five dimensions sang of all the positive possibilities in the Summer of
Peace and Love,
like both Charlies proved it was not to be
in that same hour, which belonged to the monster who bathed with me
he created the damaged new me—who I came to hate to be,
for the creature left me on that mid-summers morning...

                                only a horrid childhood memory

A MOIST WET MORNING

sitting within a solitude morning, staring upon a tiny evergreen pond
pondering life's needs and longings
behold a pintsize dewy Nymph appeared before me

curious thoughts upon curious welcomings
made my reasoning defective indeed
perhaps a prelude of urges anew in me was the reasoning

watery womanchild of tender greetings
her pixy's heart leads the way to our
puddling about misty pools of April showers

babbling putterings echoes
as nearby hares took no note
a fumbling sweeping hands dare I wisp
upon whiffed honeysuckle curls and pleasing petite curves

5 and 30 spans it seems only yesterday
this lilly pad muse of perfection was created
our stellar souls now under dewy spring spells
we lose control to lucid ageless petrified woods

upon massive mossy rocks uncontrollable desires swell
returning our play to exploring splashed boundaries that are drowned away
water ill-gotten fires we are burning into one-hundred glow-worms' glow
like magical muskrats at play we stir the waters mud

Michael Butkovich

Woe! come dividing paths with beckoning sounding alarms
sorrowful partings within acoustic awakenings invades us
with reality
forced retreat Marches me back into twilight beddings
with lingering daze upon dreamt goose feathers

a stolen cyclops glance back only reveals
a misty dissipate glimmer of the elf Nymph's flight away
never to return within a pressing day's ray

this lucid union is now locked deeply away within my hearts
vault
where visiting green fairies temp me every now and again
yet tis' the fluid Pixie of whose fragrance drippings haunts
this slumberous one
come early dewy dawns that forever i treasure

forever she swims within the milky memories
of my aging youth, the water's Nymph succubus
of a long ago…of a moist wet morning.

CATE'S EYES

Michael Butkovich

GYPSY STARE

In empty thoughts I looked about, catching sight of your Gypsy stare.
In reading of my Darken soul, fearfully you turn away.
Did you peer in too deep, that you witnessed all the Twisted layers of me?
Oh! What a Romantic novel it be, if you came to me upon a blacken moon.
What tales of horrors thereafter be, of bed-sheets bleeding come the Midnight hour.
Cries of evil carnal deeds would scream out as our Unnatural acts exceed.
We'd dance a forbidden Sabbath, partaking of potions of our own creations.
Before the dawn I'd leave you Resting, within the puddles of Sacrilegious offerings.
Wearing a fleshly made straightjacket, I'll make my escape slithering about Chapels gate.
Your dripping Skin will warm me nicely, as I button-up your stiff fingers tightly.
Is this what you foreseen when you gazed into me, is it all too Fiendishly surreal?
Perhaps tis' only the Hallows season that brings out the demented in me.
But it's from an equally disturbing Soul, that your sultry come-hither stare beckons me.
Can it be I have found at last, a fiend as depraved as myself?
Are you the one I've been seeking out, in offering me an eternal Sanctuary, Sealing me forever, within your Romani Stare…?

STOIC LIPS

Joaquin Castillo

ALTAR

The heavy dusk brings
Down your Autumn Sun

Pink clouds give way
To a Moon
New to a
Night without You

Eyes weighed heavy
Gold coins
Cover
Star-specked windows

Your voice faded
Silence only
Broken by sea salt
Sobs raising chests

Rose water perfume
Ripped from our lungs
Now thick fumes of
Burning incense

A warm smile replaced
By saintly candles
Prayers disguised
As wax-rich glass

We call out on
Bent knee
Polishing rose beads
Clenched close

Bake fresh
Your favorite foods
Sip
Your favorite drink

Beckon home
To a sacred space
Mapped by
Mexican Marigold

But you have settled
With the Ash

Jamie Crosswhite

LIVED IN

Poured flesh over bones,
Dipped skin in opinions,
Called myself anything but beautiful.
Yet, my womb housed souls
Sprouted them within me
And potted them in bedrooms next to mine;
Wildflower scent clings to my nostrils,
Hidden under sheets of memory.

When their eyes opened, I called them morning,
Their screeching rooster cries beckoning me
From bed, and the rest I once knew.
Traded quiet for beautiful chaos.
For now...for now, I am lived in. Still.
From the outside in,
Fingers and sighs and loves, grasp,
Holding tight to these roots which bore them.

Abdomen gone, from tent house to sleeping mat,
Stained with red finger paint and fiery tempers,
They outgrew my skin.
Not within, but never without.
My children find band-aids in the shelves of my eyes,
Duct-tape in the nuzzle of my chin on their ribs,
They have grown enough to check the temperature
Of *my* temperament.

Though they have bloomed, my children,
They still live in this house.

My soul ebbs out
And waters their growing muscles
Their beating hearts
Their kitten-tails, and their flame-flowers,
Teaching them the seasons
That build a sturdy, but beautiful house.

Dorielys Cruz

MONSTERS

you all exist so that
predators may consume you
and I devour *them*.

it is a game
of ticking time.
imagine being created
in His image
only to be better
stronger
faster.
dare I say smarter?

my heart has never beat in song
and the blood that runs
through my veins has
never belonged to me.

now, having freed myself
from the grasp of those
who do not wish to see
the cold, the truth, the unknown,				I roam.

Alexandra Daggett

OCEANS

>you; dreaming—
>asleep
>at home—
>probably
>of the sea
>and
>every grain of sand that
>absently
>slips through your fingertips
>
>alone
>under royal blue sheets,
>like midnight against
>rose,
>fingers tangled in lurid
>wavy hair,
>wishing you were
>here
>below
>
>hands skim
>my neck as they
>drift down
>over my stomach,
>to hips, and
>back up
>
>I think of my mouth
>on your soft,

Alexandra Daggett

of the pressure of your palms
navigating along silver,
imagine the shadow
of your breath over
my skin, and
shiver

Loverra Di Giustino

BEETLE

Ugly and alone
I crawl along the wet earth
a beetle
a black thing
that frightens

Three times you offered me a warm bed
and like a fool
I reject your embrace
I cannot believe you love a
disgusting creature like myself

Eventually I will make a
nasty crunch, shattered by your lover's foot
until then I will dwell in the soil
in the muck with all the dregs
feeding off maggots, dung and snails

You dreamed me once to be a butterfly
with wings like works of art
striking colors that reflect the sun
delicate and feminine

But I am a vermin
both predator and prey

An onyx armor safeguards my pathetic wings
the only amazement comes from wondering
how little wings could carry such a heavy load

You must love vile things
watch as I consume this ant
I bite off its head
a warning to you

And still you call me
and so I do
I fly into your line of sight

Only to be eaten by a bird

DROWNING LATE NIGHT CUES

With your smile because you still look that good
Beauty floated up by assumptions
And bulldozed by fear
I hid myself amidst imaginary trees
Smoked those leaves until the hurt seemed no more
Ashes from my jealousy marred your downy soft
Drowning late night cues
Oceans I dive under
Neck muscles knot as fist fall
Angry thoughts from my mouth to yours
You sucked them in
Shine did your aura from the attention
Then you wallowed to make my guilt bloom
You shrunk and I watched no more
But thought about all the ways to knock your spirit back
Bruises stapled to your chest
Decaying mammary glands that thrice nursed life
Weepy eyes cut glances then bounce back
Heartache oh so much can't feel my feet
Just because it happened doesn't make it so
Hold your tongue
Fold your arms
Shatter glass on paper not in real time
Punch yourself and cry I made you do it
Lay down and take it
Take it
Take it
Take it like a man
My beautiful feminine corpse

HOLY CAUCASIAN

Wobbly emotions emerge then fall;
they sink like boulders into the ocean.

Atoms split as your hook bloodies my spine—
wispy trails of purple float to the surface.

With that first breathe of air
I devour your handsome face, long legs
and fisherman arms.
I am punch drunk.

Caucasian lover I am blanketed in your world—
cocooned in white oppression
nourished by black rage.

Yes, take my denuded fish tail and wings.
So smitten with your cheekbones
I jump into your bucket.
My pride—
soggy under your brow.

You mock my deformed backbone
and cough out sizzling grease.

I want you unfettered
disown your privilege.

For your mouth.
I peel back my skin
The pain snuffed out
By the verity of your paleness.
Bite me like a cantaloupe.

I arch my back
jerk and coo;

My secretions mushroom
coating your tongue—
juices so twangy you vomit
rose petal flavored acid.
Finally,
I am your equal.

My toes curl into your flesh;
I drink in your exhalations
tasting your tongue, cheeks and teeth.

Hung

Angels come with melanated irises
that fill their sockets.
Their words scratch out my joy—
they shout that I am not worthy of my race
and bid me to leave your holy bed.

I will never let you go.

Loverra Di Giustino

MOTHER

Angry trees bite the sky,
I kick the ground as if it's
my mother's face.

This woman soils us.
She picks and prods at our belly buttons and souls.
She's a cockroach
even a corpse can't stop her.
She will not relent
until we mirror her fantasy of the white children next door.

I stride along with big werewolf steps.
I pass through the suburb
where nature is enveloped in
front porch gray, pebble gray, sidewalk gray—
green square bushes hold it down.

My mind waffles and dreams of apple batter cake,
those sparse, pleasant morning with only she and I.

Reality burns holes into my scalp,
I watch as my lips curdle on the cement;
all is burnt umber and espresso.

I will not hold my heart for forgiveness.
Nor wait for hope to sit on my tongue
and pull my cheeks up into a tiny bow.
Now is now.

I am dogged.
My tears trail back to those thoughts of colors;
mauve, tangerine, dandelion and indigo.

I sit on bony thighs and blow out my birthday candles,
the clown bending dogs and pirate swords.
While in the cut daddy harpoons the meat,
till a sweet dusky smoke hazes the air
and scratches my eyes.
Grandpa and Ma screw their faces
at the ice cream fisted children.

The clouds frown as my mood blackens.
I cannot reverse my thoughts,
or stop myself from regurgitating the past.
I am all arms and gapped teeth.

The front steps cave in and blubber,
mad ties and stiff neck mourners take my mother away
as her dog rolls around on the floor till the uncles come in
with pistols;
they threaten the weather.

I brandish my gun,
and take comfort in the bang.

Loverra Di Giustino

MOUTH HYPER

    Definitely not a Jeff
    Shaved
    Sprung
    Course black fibers soil the basin
    Pull meat back until none
    Hairless triangle
    Sashay, twirl round the room
    Diana Ross naked in red heels
    They cackle under foot
    I try to pay imagined hecklers no mind
    Bedazzled eyes sparkle blue and gold glitter
    Make the world, "I said muthafucka miss behave."
    Hegemonic episodes throw shade
    Bell pepper lips blow kisses
    Googly eyes
    Neck pop ma Walmart mirror
    Reflection all like spill the tea
    Fantasy swallowed raw
    "I love you Becky."
    Tongue taste out words untrue
    Hot sauce ragu
    Insert generic hungry nubbed lover
    Chipped palms rub over flat breast and pancake hips
    Isolation brittles dreams though, "Don't cha know?"
    Molly ain't brown
    Hard guise disguises this guy
    Toes claw magic slippers
    Appetite releases gnarled moans
    I hiccup more
    Ravenous thrust
    Suck testosterone lips
    Opposite's stubble chafe between nose and upper lip

Enjoy open mouth on mouth
Lick lick
Savor hard palate little licks
Wet muscle accent sweet nothings
Slides over sweetheart's Adam's apple
Squeezed
Lust bursts and spills over like a grape between teeth
Sizzle
Snap
Laid out on my back
Yoked limbs twerk in the sheets
Whoop
Grab
Squat and lunge
Dense bone
Smell ass
Soaked in sweat and cum
Butt
Butt But…
These groping fists are my own
Knotted weapons
Courage if had luck would eat two Big Macs and strangle out all hurt until death took me
Mildew maggot pie
Temples ache in wait
Somebody caress me
That isn't me.

Loverra Di Giustino

RUN QUEEN

    Everything you own in two trash bags,
    but you're gorgeous money
    make that honey,
    let those dollars roll and roll
    like the wheels of a Hennessey Venom GT.

    Fast cars fly past fast asses—
    queens strung out on cheap sex.
    The city soils the last bits of their dreams—
    their mouths raw from work.

    The street is an ashtray for endless drags;
    as rich tighty whities haggle for a deal.
    The onlookers cut themselves on sharp lines;
    their eyes trail over long legs that stretch out
    fishnets and flamingo pink stockings.

    Thick yellow lines divide like lips
    that bend and moan.

    "Hey dog, she's just a child."
            But John don't care.
    Her ponytails and frilly socks
            stashed away in the alley somewhere.
    Perhaps someone will find it…
    except the garbage man comes twice a week,
    three times if it's a holiday.

Here comes Cupcake,
A wig with two tube socks—
razor bumps always tarnish that coconut skin.
He slides that palm to cheek,
because it's only fifteen dollars for glass,
and free body bags at the clinic.

It's a good night for a lady,
sad night for a queen.
Run sweetie run.

Chelsea Nguyen

BLUNT BLADE

It cuts like a blunt blade on thick leathery skin.
Slices with absence of oozing blood,
so she swallows the blade
until she can't taste the blood that drains it away.

She sniffs from the table,
the scent of glorifying shame
that fills with residues of yesterday.
Hurt no longer linger, truth no longer haunts.

Each inhalation rots her organs.
Each injection contaminates her veins.
Within seconds, death is a blur
as she sits in a trance and unbreakable limbs.

He's in the warmth of the angels,
the angels who took him away,
away from the dark void she sinks into,
like quicksand in her mouth as she gasps for air.

Time after time, he yearns
for the woman who brought him to life.
The one that tells him she'll come back
each night she leaves and seldom returns.

His teary eyes and pouty lips,
chase after her as she reaches for the dust.
The dust that takes her away,
guided by a glimpse of heaven and hell.

He sits with the angels,
heart pounding for her.
His silence screams for crackling sounds
of twitching doorknobs and creaking screws.

It cuts like a blunt blade on thick leathery skin.
Slices with absence of oozing blood,
so she swallows the blade
until his eyes bring her to life.

Teja Dusanapudi

A JUMBLE OF ROCKS AND STONES IN YOUR THROAT

this is a reflection,
like your face by the lake
or the window. to see
is to be seen; watch
your expression
in the rubble of language.

watch:
repeat the mountains in your mouth. *Him
alayas*, *Andes*, *Ad-i-ron-dacks*. your lips
do not break and
your teeth do not splinter.
it is the tongue which erodes
the word mountain: say *Atlantic,* deep and slick.

let the mountains repeat you:
bleed in every soil,
cut in the skin, kiss its stone lips
and say your name:
Everest.

did you die on this page
coming up from the earth? did you linger
and will you stay, watching, choking
on the stones in your mouth? The gurgles
sound like waves.

watch:
we are the softest echoes of the sea. we are not
the voice or its silence. never
speak of it again. we scream the
mountains now. run outside
cut off your clothes
and say *Appalachian* and maybe this
time you will feel the
soil, dark and sweet, as it spills from your open mouth.

Elyse Guziewicz

LITANY

I don't sleep anymore, legs folded
across my swivel chair, drumming patterns
on the counter covered with river-mud. You
never believed me. I told you I've got
natural disasters and prisons and broken bones,
nerves are shot full of the fire in my tongue,
fragments all Greek all stuck between
my teeth, incandescent lights and cults at my heels,
pretty little thing turned gnarled by cold.

Mary Halfmann

A LUMP IN HER OATMEAL

Sometimes beneath the train tracks of my mind,
    I remember a time when Mary Friel-Blakey, my
    grandmother, and I lived together until at
    77, her mind rapidly went stealth and derailed,
    wrecking her Pullman, stopping her lights from flashing,
    and turning her circuits to mush. And how
    at three a.m. every morning, she'd rise
    again from the dead to squeeze sausage-
    style into girdle, raise snapping turtle
    garter belts over plump white thighs, line up
    the black line of silk hose, dress to hilt with matching
    designer dress, hat, shoes, purse for eight a.m. Catholic
    Mass at blue-blooded St. Patrick's Cathedral
    in Alamo Heights, Texas asking grandfather
    by four a.m., "Did I wake up late and miss Mass?"
Sometimes beneath the train tracks of my mind,
    I remember the times in the hours before mass, when
    my grandmother introduced me to her dead parents and I
    met her dead blind aunty who wasn't really blind anymore
    and how she asked me to fix all of them a sandwich and how
    her mother liked sour cream and butter on her sandwich.
    During these twilight hours Grandmother would retell the
    story of how one December night, in Letterkenny, County
    Donegal, Northern Ireland, her mother, Bridgett Yerry-Friel
    bedded down on hay inside a one-room barn, and how sheep,
    goats, and other farm animals traveled miles to greet her,
    and how by dawn her mother was blue-dead-cold,
    and how a border collie named Fiona kept her
    warm, cleaned her, fed her, and raised her

Mary Halfmann

>after her father James Friel died of a broken heart
>two months after her mother's death.
Sometimes beneath the train tracks of my mind,
>I remember the time when I was three and grandmother
>taught me to box to see if I was a lefty. The lessons paid off
>as we mimicked boxing stances at family reunions and
>grocery stores to get what we wanted without uttering a
>word. We would stomp gingerly with our right foot into
>a solid patch of space, draw back our left hand into a fist,
>stomp-rock towards the right until the target
>caved in, we scored, and could then relax and collect.
>At funerals, we would stand stoically together as a grand
>mother-granddaughter ensemble boxing team as a way to
>comfort one another. On school nights, I remember hiding
>behind the couch to listen to her eat ice or crack pecans with
>her teeth as we watched World Wide Boxing, the national
>sport of Ireland that came on at ten thirty after Dan Cook
>gave the local sports scores.
The most important thing that
my grandmother ever taught me was that having a lump in
one's oatmeal could ruin your entire day;
But, if you're Irish, you get over it.

GASLIGHTING: A CATECHISM OF EGG SHELLS

Gaslighting: To manipulate (someone) by psychological means into questioning their own sanity.

Pete's mom treated her son better than her own husband,
    and that made all the difference for the women who
    followed, seeking to please him by not stepping on egg shells.
Mary's mom liked Pete because he was Catholic Italian like her,
    dreaming of dark-eyed male babies with shiny black hair,
    who she'd groom to grow up to be just like her sons.
Mary liked Pete because he reminded her of the times her dad
    took up residency on the moon, making her believe
    if she became perfect, daddy would reward her with an
    earthly visit.
Pete called Mary's sausage-casing, egg-shell-breakfast-tacos defective
    and made her believe that she was as flawed as those tacos
    as the hair on his bathroom floor was not from another
    woman.
Pete showed Mary how to crack eggs with a spoon, deposit yolks
    into the blender for eggnog milk shakes.
    And they studied with a priest to pass their nuptials.
They took turns doing a year of neither-here's-nor-there's.
    When he was off, she was on. When he left, she stayed,
    permanently turned on, connected to his neither-here's-nor-there's.
They parted, with his saying, "You scare me, I can't satisfy you,
    you nasty woman, you old hag, you lesbian bitch."
    Her thinking, "All this to keep your egg shells intact?"
She learned to crack eggs with her feet and dreamed of
    him smashed cock-stiff-dead as the baby chick
    she lost at Easter when she was five.

Mary Halfmann

The walls of her bedroom mostly naked now,
>   she replaced the loin cloth of the crucifix that dangles over
>   her king-sized bed with a Michael Phelps Speedo.

THE GIRL THEY CALLED SKELATOR IN LAKE-HILLS, TEXAS

The local constabulary sits at the four-way. There's only one
way in and one way out
    of Lakehills, Texas unless you're a tweaker and able to fly
out mentally, you have to pass Ernie Right parked under the shabby
        oak tree at the corner of Highway 1283 and Texas Park Road
        37.
Too early for lunch, Ernie logs into the hotspot of local realtor, Karen Ripley,
    to see if his paycheck has been deposited at the Wells Fargo
across the street. Satisfied, he fiddles with the squelch on his
police radio, adjusting
        the volume down, flying his left arm half-mast outside of his
        patrol car
to signal locals that he's friendly today, and not in cat and
mouse police activity mode.
    He stares at his lap, covers his Glock with his right hand and
    falls asleep.
At 1037 hours the Bandera Dispatcher puts out an APB missing
person report
    on a Tiffany Smith AKA Skelator, Caucasian female, 18,
    missing front teeth,
long silver hair, hazel eyes, 5'6" 80 pounds last seen on Halloween
two Fridays ago
    at Apizza Mia wearing Wolf's Den tank top, filthy, baggy
    ripped jeans.
Thursday's lunch special at La Cabana is chicken puffy tacos. Roxanne,
    Ernie's favorite waitress, reminds him of Selena, a dead pop
    star.
He sits at one of her tables and stares at her chest until she jokes with

him: "Hold the
> beans, don't cut the cheese, *Cortar las judías no el queso.*"

Ernie had known Skelator since she waddled like a little milk truck toddler. Last week,
> he watched her noodle walk into the EzMart, buy a can of Redd's Ale and

a Southern Cut pack of Marlboros. Back on patrol, he realized even though she
> looked like a grandmother, she couldn't be a day over 18.

Lakehills was abuzz with the news. Everyone had a police scanner, and for days,
> the first thing uttered by one citizen to another was, "Have you seen Skelator?"

Skelator had stopped showing up at the community Monday night meal at the Lakehills
> Methodist Church. Someone there noted that perhaps Skelator was dead.

The next morning, the locals greeted one another with, "Have you seen Skelator?"
> The automatic reply to the greeting was "She's probably dead."

A month later, I saw Skelator giving flying lessons in front of Altek Elementary
> on 1283 a mile past the four-way. Nobody's seen her since.

Karen Hatfield Cisneros

POSED

Nicholas Kelley

AND IF YOU ASK GANYMEDE?

> —who is unbridled Jupiter
> Cyrus Cassells, "*Atavism*"

My babe don't go. He gimme all the fits and all the feels—you know. He soakin' up the sun at high noon. He do me real nice—it's true. He all over the spectrum, he hues of carnal. His thighs are the altar that I pray to now. Blank the pages, written by ages that carved me in stillness, 'cause my body cage-less. I been set ablaze, caught in his gaze.

Our firm embraces—faces-to-faces—we take turns, trade places and turn tail, tail chasin' love. We tear up the place and still need more space. We shoot past the moon and smash up all the stars swaddled in stellar swoon. He and me—draped-in-cosmic-light like—we drink the galaxy dry. A black hole cleanse is better when he and I are nape to chin, lit up and drunk on dead suns. We burstin' at the seams tonight and we Big-Bang-blowin' new skies.

Sigh contagious, come-down in stages, we burn off ourselves, and fall into our places. I watch as we cool in our silk-sheet sweat-pool. Young and naked, drenched in new day dust, he hold onto me, he my tangled kite string. I'm flyin' and dazed as he rains his praise down on me.

Emerson Little

CHANGES

Emerson Little

JAILED HOPES

Raquel Lopez

YELLOW BLISS

Osamah Mandawi

AFTER THE SHIP WENT DOWN

SS Carl D. Bradley, Michigan: Structural Failure, Brittle Steel

I kissed my mother's pale cheek
and left my home this morning.
I took the death letters and let the wind toss me
across the streets like an orphaned leaf.

I couldn't sleep a wink last night because I was getting tortured
by clouds screeching the blackboard sky
outside my window, as they left the storm.

For 31 years, it was a cargo ship.
Now, it's rusted steel left beneath the waves,
like a paper letter covered in the tears
of the 23 dead ship crew members that died last night.

I stood up straight, or at least I tried
gently knocked on the door,
a boy, behind him a storm,
and an envelope in his hand.
I tried to stand but the wind swayed
me out of place, like a curtain.

MEMORIES IN OVERHEAD BINS

I remember feeling a clean tile floor
under my Timberland knockoff Iraqi boots,
entering through an open door
a well-lit carpeted room, and taking a seat
right beside my baba because I had to.
There were no chains between our seats,
but I still felt stuck. Maybe I did
because the walls looked like they were covered in liquid glue.
Welcome to the United States of America!
on a printer paper, nailed to the wall,
(maybe glued). I remember
watching an airplane
from a window at the very back of the room,
as it ponders the clouds on the May-warm concrete paving.
I looked at them, and they seemed heavy
with other passengers' memories.

Osamah Mandawi

OBSERVATIONAL STUDY OF ONE TREE'S EXCESSIVE EXTROVERT BEHAVIOR

I was waiting for an email, when it hit me
That the Red Oak tree outside my window
Grows jealous, when I stare too long at my laptop screen.

It bends its branches just enough
To flash the sunshine in my face,
Like a twisting contortionist.

Some days,
It anxiously plucks off its own leaves,
Lets its own red oak blood gush.
It, aims, sighs, and throws at my window
One sacrifice,
And then another.

It never gives up.
Every now and then,
While my eyesight is smeared on the screen,
It calls on a squirrel
To crawl to my sill
And wave,
Tug on my attention,
Break my window
With some acorns
It spent hours looking for
Under all those bloodstained
Leaves from the day before.
And I just click

Reload,

Reload,

Reload.

Osamah Mandawi

ROTTEN RELIC FROM 2018

Geoffrey Welgraz of 61 years
    died of premeditated poisoning

Divorced and jobless
  couldn't even afford his son's
    25 cents corner store candy cravings

Supped sorrow
    until his stomach grew twice its size
    until blue veins of grief accumulated under
    his thin skin
    and his sadness oozed from every pore

One day in a street in Manhattan
    he chugged poison
    hunched over his steering wheel
    and succumbed in his car

The high bass radios rumbled by
  pedestrians on conveyer belts passed
    someone smelled the rot crawling
      out of the window one week later

Based on an article that appeared in print on Oct. 24, 2018, on Page A1 of the New York Times, with the headline: Dead and Passed by for Days: A Story of Despair in New York.
"Geoffrey Corbis... found in his car on a busy street in the East Village on Aug. 31, a week after he committed suicide and his family reported him missing to the local police station."

Aaron Martinez

IN A DIVE BAR AT THE END OF THE WORLD

    ten minutes till impact
    astronomers counting down
    God's on the clock
    breaking news on a Panasonic tube t.v.
    a gloom of Chanel perfume and cigarette smoke
    Jim Morrison hymns meter the blues
        in a dive bar
                at the end of the world

    another bullet-biting Angel's Envy
    another twenty in the tip jar
    half a pack of Parliaments left

    finding a siren's reflection in broken glass
    she's a pale brunette sipping Belvedere
    and crossing her legs
    "Light My Fire" lost in translation
    vodka-chilled breath forgets
    three strangers arrested
    she and I, and
        you the bartender
            in a dive bar
                at the end of the world

Aaron Martinez

(TRANS)SEXUAL

In high school I hid away,
hiding cheap Maybelline mascara
and BH blush under my bed,
dreaming one day I'd whisper Lady Danger,
a vision to Lure in Lower Manhattan.

I kept my own company, filling notebooks
with sketches of sequined dresses, portraits
of beautiful women I watched, gliding
over marble steps, disappearing like angels
in a whirlwind of diamonds at the Met Gala.
I envied them. I didn't understand why
at the time, but I wanted to be them.

I wanted to wear the most dazzling Dior gowns,
tip-toeing in the tallest, reddest Louboutin heels,
my long wavy-golden locks lifted in the breeze
clutching an alligator-green Hermes,
clinging to the arm of a suave, worldly man
with a handle-bar mustache and a Maybach
whose musk of Shaygrueme cigar-smoke
and Lalique Hommage aftershave
envelops me.

M. C. Maxwell

A POET'S DEATH

When I die, my poems will mourn my brilliance.
They will shed transcendent tears just for me.
They will aid and carry out my
unfinished legacy.

The Odes will write my eulogy.
The Elegies will comfort my queen.
The Ballads will sing everlasting praises.

The Haikus will organize the funeral.
The Limericks will lighten the mood.
The Sonnets will sympathize each
soul.

He created us when nobody else would.
He brought us into existence, out of the
very shadows of unwelcomed thoughts.
He gave us salvation in the form of narration.

The attendants will praise my sacred name that has yet to be
honored. I hold onto these fond memories of children that
I molded. My kin reached out to me when they
were just form less ideas. I offered my sons a
place in my mind and
daughters a refuge in my
heart.

I gifted each poem with shape.
I supplied them all with sanctuary.

I received an outlook on life in return
for the life I breathed in and out again.

        With my death, poetry has a chance to
            grasp a sense of sanity and serenity.
                I am no longer terrified or afraid!
                    The land is constantly in
                      dismay.

Thank you Sire! We will never forget you!
And now the world will never forget us!

A POET'S PASSION

I excel at the intricate details, invoking the power of pathos,
abandoning the sophistication of logos and the morality
of ethos. I dedicate myself to the journey of devotion.
I synchronize with seduction. My abilities
stem from the passion inside a cavern
that shields all words and
wishes.

I form these erotic
images with tender ease,
molded by imagination's cradled
love child that the two of us innately
share. I spawn sensual symbols, passionate
personification, animalistic and exotic allegory, vivacious
visions for her like a mystical magician
performing organic wonders to
enchant and charm a broken veil.

My girlfriend always told me that the sexiest part of
my body was my brain. If only she knew the
gift of my mouth. I could make her
moan and scream with my
own elongated DIC -
tion that becomes
hard.
My voice holds vast
a choir, a choir of ten
thousand personas, each withholding
a unique story to tell and retell, cherishing
a collection of moments. She loves to listen like a
Desdemona in need of a darling and daring Othello.

Maxwell Meier

My fasciation ignited a miraculous transformation. All I am is a poet
seeking more ways, weapons to aid my crusade, craving a
wild fantasy with my maiden and minx. We prepare
ourselves for the realms that mother the
chaos, the creatures, and the written
creations I have yet to frame
like moist
incantations.

My thirst for adventure progresses.

Emil Meila

AFTER AUERBACH

Emil Melia

GIRL GHOST

HOW I CURED MY TRICHOTILLOMANIA

I could cut all my limbs off
Give myself a handmade haircut
Instead of picking myself apart
I could probably go away
Give everywhere a piece of my mind
Give everywhere a piece of me
A strand of hair for you…and a strand of hair for you…

All my power is in my right hand
I've had visions of smashing things all day
If I could translate it from fingers to fists
If I could regrow in seconds
Slowly rebuilding in rest but little pinpricks of day
Repeated relentless removal in waking
Will never get rid of her completely

SELF IN SEA

SELF PORTRAIT WITH YELLOW ROSES

Emil Melia

SHH…YOU'VE BEEN PREPARING FOR THIS ALL YOUR LIFE

I had barbed wire for breakfast.
An utterly shredded esophagus and
These shrinking lungs will still take weeks to heal and disappear
I never asked for these or those grabbing hands
Though I had been preparing for this all my life
Primed and prepped and toned like canvas and skin
At what age did I become sentient?

Home&Church&School&Sundayschool
No one said a word, the only clear instruction
Sinful, shameful: Go To Confession
Smother yourself in that heavy velvet curtain and
Come out when you're clean
Some choke to death every week
As ancestral saints and gargoyles look down in proud disdain
Fasting for the Eucharist
Starving for a comfortable breath but
This practice is our only inheritance
It can only take one wrong confession to be
Written out of the will

Dexter Morales

1942

Did something about me suddenly change
In the mist of the night?
                                      I still look the same in the mirror.

Nazi forces were rounding us all up,
what really made us different I do not know.
                                      We are not animals on a farm.

Germany was my original home, but
we had to leave when I was four.
                                      Home was to never be seen again.

Father said it was the best plan for
the family. Amsterdam would now
be the place we call home. At least for
the next two years, of my remaining few.
                                      1945 would be the start to my end.

I missed playing outside with friends, but
now my only escape was my imagination.

                              And the noises I heard through the walls.

A dairy full of blank pages was my birthday gift,
it would become by best friend.

                              My lasting impression on the world.

Gabriella Pawelek

OLD CUSTOMS / OVER THE OUIJA BOARD

I said, "The woods."
He said, "A dark room. A black candle. Two of us."
It didn't matter so
I let him have his way.
Three circles in the middle, then he winks,
"Should we kiss?"
The entire alphabet before us,
but he moves the planchette up to "Yes."
and ignored all the spirits.
The candle didn't even quiver as much
as his shaking teenage hand.
That's not how you play.

    My grandmother was a witch.
    She had tarot cards, Ouija boards, things in jars.
    For three years, I was the only one who visited.
    My mom said, "That's not my mother in there."
    I said, "It's her, you just didn't know her very well."
    Sometimes, she'd ask me to wheel her down to the woods,
    and she'd have me smoke a joint with her.
    "Curative properties," she'd explain.
    When she was high, she told me, laughing
    that she killed my grandfather long ago.
    They were married before she was eighteen.
    She didn't love him but
    it didn't matter so
    she let him have his way
    many times, before she smarted up. She told me,
    it was an old custom. They didn't know what they know now.

Gabriella Pawalek

A dark room. A black candle. Two of us.
It's an old custom to kiss boys you don't want to kiss,
but my grandmother was a powerful witch
and she killed the man who liked tradition.
"Well?" he says.
It's not how you play,
        But this matters so
                I moved the planchette to "Goodbye."

Kelci Piavis

ALLEN GINSBERG

       pulled me in like a
       trap door spider,
encircled me with
arachnid legs made
       with dreams, with drugs,
       with waking nightmares
       alcohol and cock and
       endless balls.
Jewish Communist fag
fighting the endless dynamo of

       capitalist tendencies:
       taking my money,
       throwing it at
fortune 500s—just to
look cool—
but blowing joint smoke
in the face of that
fucking capitalist pig we call
president.

       oh, ginsberg
       oh, man of beat
what would you say if you saw
neo-nazis in the street
a business man running the
country
gay marriage legalized
a black former president

        who admitted to smoking weed
        (he is one of us)

i may not be
old enough to see
the best minds of my generation
be destroyed
        but old enough to see the process.
        heroin and opioid overdoses—
        what ever happened to
        Peyote and marijuana and
        acid, lsd,
even cocaine snorted
off a stripper's ass
is safer.

Victoria Ramirez Gentry

ALWAYS AFTER

It's not like losing an arm or a leg,
it's like someone stole the blankets from my bed
on a winter night, when the cold creeps
in through the cracks of my windows

and clasps my bones. It's not like someone ripped
out my heart, it's like someone removed my lungs, but
my body continued to move—my heart
continued to beat—gasping for air

but never able to breathe. It's like someone tapped
my shoulder, but when I look, no one's there.
It's when I visit my family for Christmas,
or I eat dinner with my friends and I think I'm happy—

I laugh—but it cuts my throat and I
swallow the blood and silence down
to my stomach where it churns.
It's not like—It's wanting to hold her tight,

but she's deep in the ground.

Victoria Ramirez Gentry

WAKE

    Where hands once touched, skin
    now regrows—all forensic traces of him
    gone. *"You're going to be okay"* someone—
    everyone—tells her & she reaches but cannot grasp

    the word that slides through the cracks
    in her fingers like golden grains of sand,
    collecting in a mound, encased by glass,
    marking the march of time. She sits,

    a student in class, she walks
    to the bus stop—her eyes glance—aware
    of every moving body & rippling
    muscle beneath skin lit

    by the sun—lungs expand—& she watches
    unfurling fingers, dirt beneath their nails.
    She wakes in a soaked bed,
    waxy skin & dry mouth, flinging

    limbs to fight the phantom hands
    lingering
    on her thighs. She laughs with her friends
    swallowing toast & eggs for brunch, wincing

    at the glare of the stained-glass windows
    from the church across the street—the colors echo
    the night that speckled her arms & legs
    black & green. She cannot pretend

    away her lacerated flesh,

pink & chafed, healing in jagged scars
no one sees. She wets the sand with salty tears,
grips "okay" & holds
the word in her fingers.

Xavier Reyna

GOD IS...

found in the poems of loving madres,
their tender words heal bones y kiss
eyelids, but also enlighten ignorance.

found in el feo arte de ASCO,
defiantly resting, unforgotten, on the
ghostly skin of a face that rejects pigment.

found in ancient pools of bloody ink,
ceremonially etched into holy bodies
by a shaman who understands numbers.

found in the space between sound,
often misunderstood pero jamás taken
for granted, maestros channel heaven.

found in the blankets on our backs,
stitched y crafted by firm hands that
have kept babies y abuelos warm for centuries.

found in the sketchbooks of niños y niñas,
there lay divine images from spirits
who don't speak the language of this earth.

to the unnamed artist,
thank you.

POEM FOR MY FATHERS

    i ran under a full moon's pulse and i felt
    my grandfather jogging next to me like he
    used to do when he was young like me,
    i heard he could press cuatrocientos
    libras over his head like it was nada,
    scar your thighs with twigs and leaves
    fend off evil spiritualities with a glance
    teach you the lord's many teachings
    feed a family with a broken back,
    these are some of the things i've heard
    and i carry his name inside my blood.

    i heard my father's sharp voice waterfall
    a story of a funeral that left him broken
    stories of games with other poor children
    stories of whippings from his father
    a story of how he, rugged wise clueless,
    met my mother, who'd sing to god's fields,
    and how much he loves her
    and how much he loves the stars
    and how much he loves our bones
    and how much he loves my imperfections
    and how much he loves our hearts,
    i had never heard him cry before.

Xavier Reyna

SUEÑOS DE VERANO

mi primer sueño, tú.

honey with the honey skin and grand, gorgeous
hair that both captivates and frightens me, whose
words fascinate me, and whose voice soothes me,
who are you?

mi segundo sueño, ¿qué más puedo pedir?

raspa on a sunny, hot day with the ducks.
pond clean, air crisp, sky blue, grass green,
i could stay here forever.

mi último sueño, familia.

took me twenty-one years to appreciate the beauty
of la reyna, our family name, and her unique
temperament, strengths, and weaknesses.

it's filled with love, pride, vitality, and grit.
our bond is rooted and firm and grows stronger and
more meaningful as each of us grows stronger.

from the garden to casa grande to there and here,
we'll be together forever and always

UNTITLED 13

my defense mechanism is
mucho machismo in the lies i secrete

when you ask me if i've ever been in love
and i fake like i haven't,
when you speak to me in my native tongue
and i fake like i understand,
when you offer me a dollar and change
and i fake like i don't need it,
when you offer me your company
and i fake like i don't want it,
when you say i have a contagious smile
and i fake like i'm not depressed,
when you diagnose me with you phd
and i fake like i'm not depressed.

my defense mechanism is
mucho machismo fronting over tears

when thoughts of suicide warm my
chest like aged irish whiskey,
when my bank account is reminiscent
of our section eight housing,
when anxiety is compressing both my
lungs inside of a kimura,
when a friend invites me to their function
and i don't leave the house,
when a woman invites me out dancing
and i don't leave the house,
when my aging pops y madre tell me
they love me.

Brianna Schunk

LATERAL KNOTS

    i pay to pass
    this place.
    spirit persists
    permit me peace.
    push past pain pills
    push & pull
    push & pull
    palliate shoulder blades.
    only palms placed
    predict no future
    lament no past.
    pull me present
    peppermint oil & pain.

MY BODY IS NOT A FLOWER

my body is not a flower
that blossoms and withers with each passing season.
the world allows no such beauty and grace
that wishes to come and go,
        come and go.

my body is not a gentle wind
that brings sweet scents of nectarine and honey.
the world allows no such season and time
that wishes to blow to and fro,
        to and fro.

    no.

my body is a gate always open
    gardens trampled underfoot
my body is granite lava
    red-hot flow however slow
my body is ocean rains
    flushed out of storm drains
my body is a restless being
    spirit on the breeze of change

the world wishes to keep us still and sedentary,
planted in the dirt,
    ignoring its own nature
        to spin around the sun.

Brianna Schunk

SPOTLIGHT

      This is not a green hillside,
      This is not mouths open wide,
      This is not running, not sprinting,
      This is not galloping, glasses glinting,
      This is not blue sky clear overhead,
      This is nothing but imagery, dead,
      This is not a sky of silver stars,
      But there is a light behind the bars.
      Watch me kneeling, struggling to stand.
      I will do anything if you let me,
      you don't understand. I'll
      Paint a smile on under the rouge
            Part the curtains and
                  Push off—

A review:
This is not hipbones clicking,
This is not jawbone sticking,
This is not knees bruising or strained,
This is not thighs burning in pain,
This is not vertebrae curving behind
    Looping up to touch an orange rind,
This is not sweat dripping down the back,
This is not ankles about to crack,
This is not perfect and long pointed feet,
This is not missing a single damn beat,
This is not blistered toes reaching two inches long,
This is not reinforced ideas known all along,
This is not a broken machine
    Angular, dripping, and full of disease,

This is not missing a choice up to make
  To demolish the limits the body can take,

This is not judging the beauty outside,
This is not about faults that are trying to hide,
This is not just disability redefined,
This is not having anything to hide behind,
Not seeking pity or prayer, but the chance
  To teach this defiant old corpse how to dance,
Hold it up, tighten an aching abdomen
  And land with grace, undefeated, and then
Exhale absolution, forgiving and sweet,
Proving unfinished bodies are just as complete,
Makeup melts off, revealing a face
That wouldn't want to be any other place.
This is not jumping with fear I might fall,
But joy that I'm able to leap after all.

Morgan Spalding

WHORE

I was 14 and he was 25   he stared in my eyes while I sat on top of him
                    he told me   I would make   a lot of money
in the strip club   a table in front of us is littered with beer cans, rolled up
dollar bills, and pills
ecstasy burns   my nostrils   I feel the vomitus taste dripping down the
back of my throat   I attempt to rinse it away with beer   I crush
pills into a fine dust   while a friend
kisses my neck
I carve the word   "whore"   in my thigh with a razor blade because that's
what they
say I am

I was 16 and he was 26   he thrusted himself into me from behind
                he told me   I was made to be a porn star   I can't re-
member how I got to his apartment   I was a runaway   it started with
me on a sidewalk and   him yelling
derogatory compliments out of a beat up civic   my hands gripped the
sheets of his bed   and   I performed for him

I was 18 and he was 39   I'm on my knees in a laundry room
                    he told me   I was too beautiful   to be on the
streets
why not dance for money?   why not I let someone take care of me?
                his
wife sleeps in the room next door   one of his hands grips my throat
the other
brushes a stray piece of hair to the side of my face

I was 19 and he was 40   I'm in a poor apartment in East Oakland
              he told me   he would make me a star   put me on
posters
if I could fuck strangers   at   "the drop of a hat"
his hands hold me into his bed by my throat
                        "no cop will come to save a whore in Oak-
land"   he said
I light cigarette after cigarette   I suck in menthol nicotine   to cut
through the numbness   of my cocaine   drenched mouth
          lighters swish into flame under piece of foil   I inhale
cops yell at me
handcuffs cut into my wrists   I roll my eyes   people stare

I was 14 and he was 25
                    we spent hours painting on walls of his garage and
writing songs together   our hands are covered in a multitude of colors
he writes poetry on the inner thigh of my jeans while I smoke a cigarette
broken guitar strings buzz behind us with a song about heroin outcasts
the room is filled with songs about
me

I was 16 and he was 26
                    we passed a bottle of whiskey around in a living room
laughing drunk with life and blurred vision   telling stories
about angels and demons and overdose

I was 18 and he was 39
                    we talked about God and family   our kids
played outside
he gazed into me   and told me he was "lost in my eyes"   we
went to church   we rolled blunts   we rolled dice

I was 19 and he was 40
                        we went grocery shopping for my daughter
he sat up at night listening to all my dreams   he hands me whiskey and
lights my cigarette   he tells me I'm the most beautiful girl in the world and
sells me to a man I've never met
that's what they say I am

Lemuel Torres

UNTITLED I

do not ever believe that you own
any of these words.
No one owns them;
not even me, they are transient angels
who have lost their way,
they are secret vision
an altar ofrenda given to me.
Don't stand there with your arms crossed
blind trying to give my words meaning,
they are endless and eternal.
Who made you god with metatronic
amplified pulpit voice to sing them back to me?
Don't ever think that my shadow belongs in a box
inside the putrid rooms where you keep your pain,
I'm walking the sky nightly asking God to come back,
I'm walking through hades dark and frozen,
I'm running from heaven yellow and burning,
drowning in sorrows and vowels.
I'm decoding incomprehensible sentences
to avoid the nightmare of paper staying
blank.
You don't own these words,
No one does.

Krystal Trlicek

I CAN REMEMBER

if I close my eyes and think really hard
I can remember some good things
Barbara
setting a jar of tea in the sun
the soothing sound that wind chimes make
laundry on clothespins
a rooster's crow
just as the sun set the morning on fire
the cool wet grass iced with morning dew
under my little bare feet

of these things I remember
I have the clearest picture
of how the light illuminated our small home
leaving no darkness from the night before
calming our fears of the night to come
we ignored Barbara's black eyes and bruised legs
we swept up glass
and when we forgot the past
we sipped our tea made of sun
enjoying a few hours of playing house

when the sun set and darkness approached again
the only light we could see was from his headlights
when we heard the gravel crunch under his tires
our stomachs would churn
our teeth would clench

not every night was awful

sometimes he would walk in smiling
and swing me around the room
but until the door opened
we had no way of knowing
what kind of night it would be

my young ears were trained
to listen for his work boots
and hope for normal rhythm
not drunken a stumble
as the lock clicked
and the doorknob rotated
I would breath in
and out
"Hi daddy"

SEVENTY-ONE PERCENT

…were male, and it is the leading cause of death in men age 20-44

Ohayōgozaimasu
morning is early
where I come from
America is sleeping
in yesterday
when my sun rises
the race begins
as soon is my feet
hit the pavement
I am one
in a sea of faces
joining in the working man's march
I glide through the station
make my body fit
behind closing doors
it was like this
yesterday
and the day before
and the day before
and the day before
I decide on a destination
Today's place to hide
I lost my job
two weeks ago
and I have yet to tell my wife
when the day ends
I go for a drink

again
It's too late to think
and then
I stumble for the train
I think about the shame
of reliving the same
yesterday
And every week without pay
Will my son be okay?
I get ready to fit
but for the first time
I don't want to fit
I am one
of seventy-one percent
the train comes in fast
I look at the doors
But then
I aim for the tracks

Emily Turner

INTERPLACE RD.

> And the terror and the horror
> God, I wonder why we bother
>
> Lorde, "Sober II (Melodrama)"

I'm waiting at a crosswalk wondering
how it is that I took two steps forward
but I am falling three steps behind.

Petrichor lingers on the asphalt
        and PAC's uproot fistfuls of grass just for fun.

Stoplights flash green for a blink
        and Red demands the next six years.

Fading stripes tattoo the road
        and a white flag singes black in my back pocket.

I'm waiting at a crosswalk staring
at the lifeless pedestrian monitor,
frustrated by the way the faint blue
image refuses to move its
        goddamn   feet.

There comes a moment when prayers will only reach as far as your
two hands and some people won't even lift
        a fucking finger.

I'm waiting at a crosswalk thinking
about the two steps forward:
        small

                    victories
of gender, race, religion, age, sexuality
        (intersectionality fought for its right in office,
        as hegemony bought its place on the throne
        it calls democracy),
of youth painting a rusty state bright purple.

Maybe it was all the sidewalk cracks
we couldn't avoid that broke Lady
Liberty's back. The torch in Her right
hand, the law in Her
left: she is powerless in the absence
of one of Her beloved objects,
but even weaker when they operate
in opposition to one another.

I'm waiting at a crosswalk stumbling
over the cracks in my voice to find
the words to console Her,
but I'm fumbling through all the noise,
caught between the two victorious steps forward
and the three steps that tug from behind.

Maybe we just forgot how to walk.

Emily Turner

SUN & STARS

Dante described divinity
in these few celestial terms:

*L'amor che move il sole
e l'altre stelle.* I looked in

the mirror this morning and I
could have sworn I watched it crack. I

asked myself how do you even
try to convince someone they are

worth all the seven continents
when they never learned to open

an atlas; how can you even
try to teach someone to breathe when

all they know is drowning? *L'amor
che move il sole e l'altre*

stelle. I wrote these words in the
cold cracks of the mirror, hoping

the same love that moves the sun and
the stars would move something in me.

I wonder: has anyone tried
weaving the sun and stars into

love? I feel so small but maybe
I'm just holding the telescope

upside down again.

Matthew Vernon

WITNESS

We climb the hill behind the house,
my master with the yearling cow and
me. The dawn-light glinting
sidelong off the heifer's glossy hide is
a memory of the morning star
reflecting its own shadow. As we
walk out past the fence gate posts
into the winter pasture (now in bloom), the gray
grass swells in the fickle breeze.
I hear the sea swells move across the grain
and splash against my side unrhythmically.

The man, who walks with purpose in his stride,
holds limply wood and steel there at his side
or shifts the load to point into the sky.
The quiet beast, chewing, climbs the hill.
From sunrise toward the falling-down.
I guess she thinks this Eden, the meadowland
unspoiled. And she the sole inheritor
of an eternal realm of hay—this paradise of grain.

But here where we can see the earth
stretch out beyond itself, we pause and tie
the yearling cow to some eternal oak.
The dawn-light in crescendo
echoes off her onyx hide. A crimson sky
offsets a gem of silver on the rise. Now
wood and steel rise coldly through
the chilled mid-morning air. Chewing she

stares down at me; blissful bovine stare.
He raises up his single arm and heavily exhales.
Her stare, now without object, falls
beside the hallowed tree
in rippling peals of thunder
that vibrate through the dew. She lies
where she belongs upon the earth,
black hide and life-blood mingle
with the dirt.

Now two descend the hill into the yard.
My master finds his way into the barn
to finish what's been done. I wrack
my mind for how she might have sinned.
I don't think I will climb that hill again.
I don't think I will climb that hill again.

Quintin Walton

PROSTITUTION TOWN

My beloved brother, Max, luckiest son of a bitch—
Immerse him naked in pig shit a mile deep,
He'll rise, a phoenix reeking of lemon verbena.
Hope Diamond clenched between his teeth,
Gold doubloons leaking from his ass.
Dad's favorite son.

As I brood, a robin redbreast taps on my bedroom shutter.
The crimson herald delivers a cryptic note from Max.
Gallivanting on his ten-speed steed across the states, Max
caught a flat.
Stranded in an out of the way little place
Off the conventional path, Prostitution Town.

Enclosed with Max's mayday, a map.
I dash quicksilver to the mysterious destination
On blind faith, my brother's keeper.
What provocative treasure has Max stumbled upon?
Flesh paradise, erotic Never Neverland?

Prostitution Town.
The titillating name worth a peek.
But I discover no Max.
No Vegas Strip or even Sodom & Gomorrah
No Amsterdam with red lights, no Sunset Boulevard.

Prostitution Town.
Pretty place, sweet air, wholesome, beautiful people.
Max wrote: look for Uncle Betty's Pie Emporium.

All this way for blue balls and quaint Ma and Pop dessert?

Throbbing curiosity propels my special purpose
Inside a sensual feast unveiled before my thirsty eyes
Teeming toned physiques, tanned nudity, male, female
Gorgeous, young, older, minimally dressed

I sidle up to the counter, occupy the only available seat
Stunned by the exposed skin, hypnotized by tantalizing aromas
Before I can order, a luscious hunk of golden-hued pecan pie materializes
The glistening musclebound server clad in a see-thru apron
I ravish the scrumptious pie; the seductive filling, the gigantic nuts
Lost in the emerald eyes of the beefcake leaning toward me
A sublime sweet after taste lingers in my mouth
The price for a slice of heaven: a Benjamin Franklin
Thanks Max.

Ronald Philip Williams

DEVIL'S WEAR

      make a girl come before you do and she's pleased because all the men in her life before you couldn't get her there smile as she's going berserk she has daddy issues and was never loved as a child so she chases love in the backseat of your mustang you're not a loving boyfriend you're a demon in disguise and she's playing with fire but you like it because the flames feel good let her suck you off to interludes of rain and she doesn't love you but she's almost there so you let her believe you're falling for her too so you can keep using her on nights like this and it's exactly how you want things to be but you cry when she leaves

FALLEN

A pickup truck could rush its headlights into my spine today and I wouldn't feel any different.
Maybe it'll elevate me high enough so the sky could start giving me some answers.
Eyes closed,
mind wide-open,
and a heart falling behind me for someone who actually has the arteries to use it.

LAUREN'S INTERLUDE

    You took me for a drive in your maroon Scion. I remember thinking you were more of an SUV kind of girl but there you showed up in this little racecar-looking machine ready to roll. I strapped myself in before I noticed your vibrant red lips. Perfect and full. The kind of lips that tell lies and deceive men like me into thinking they can actually have you.
    "Hey you."
    "You always say that."
    "I'm always me."
    You grinned and pulled the gear-shift back. We trailed on highways that seemed much brighter than they had been before. Lane strips began to look a lot more like lines of cocaine rather than separated coats of paint. I felt calm, yet uneasy due to how safe I felt with you. We're not a conventional pair. We're demons disguised as angels so that God won't banish us. I kept thinking, "You have me wrapped around your finger you know."
    "I doubt that."
    "Ah, the almighty pessimist."
    "No, really. You could've responded every time I reached out but you never did. If that's your definition of having you wrapped around my finger, then we need to reconsider the terms."
    I hated how witty you were. I loved how witty you were.
    "I've got the papers in my back pocket. Would you like to renegotiate now or under more familiar circumstances?"
    You laughed an honest laugh. The kind that made me smile to hear it. Your white teeth gleamed beneath your lips and I hated how infatuated I was by the sight of you. The music ranged from lo-fi interludes to alternative guitar melodies and sounds. I became drunk off the way the music complemented the passing imagery—some dark highway with no lights in sight, only forest trees and open lands in the distance. Your hand reached over for mine and you hesitated

when you felt how cold I was.

"You're always so cold!"

"And you *always* say that."

The drive was originally designed to be a tour of your new area but somehow we ended up in the parking lot of your old high school. What started in the passenger seat and lead to the back of your car became the fuel to every pump I ignited. As your mouth opened wider than one should and my hand against the frigid window, I couldn't get enough of the glamour that is you. Fucking you is poetry. Your body moved like a snake, and your dark hair fell perfectly over your eyes like the vibrance of us was too dreamlike to witness. But you weren't dreaming. You pushed your body on top of mine, both hands around my neck. Choking was your thing, and I could've died right then, but even if I had I would've convinced God you were still the angel he thought you to be.

YOUR HEART IS BEATING

"I need you to put both of your hands on my chest."
"I can't feel anything."
"I didn't expect you to."
"Then why make me put them here?"
"I need you to understand I don't feel because I don't want to, I don't feel because I can't."
"I wouldn't believe that even if you did."

She plucked me into her by my lower back, hung her arm around my neck, and stared up at me with the brightest stars in her eyes. Her lips slightly opened like lips do after an hour of watching the most dramatic film.
I wanted to kiss her. More than anything in this moment. Before the thought took action,

"Don't."

She raised her heels to neutralize our mouths and drew closer. It seemed like a reflex to close my eyes.
I felt like I'd just leaped into the deep-end of a neighborly pool, fighting the chlorine.

Her tongue traced around my mouth, pulling away with my bottom lip beneath her teeth.

A hand removed, an arm unhung, open eyes.

She'd vanished.

Away from my daydreams, away from my mind. I opened my eyes again, and I'd never felt such a burn that blinking couldn't cure.

(Beat)

Anjelica Zapata

DIRTY THOUGHTS: BETTER TO BE LEFT UNHEARD, UNREAD

I'm silent as the waters get rough,
The winds grow strong and everyone's voices
For once fall silent.
Clouds above me,
Try to remind me,
Dear me, there is a Sun
be appreciative of the occasionally hard, overwhelming rain.
Then I begin to think,
what if?

What if I just lift my head
open my mouth
and taste the pain of everything?

Just until I can't think
Until my mind, heart, and body flood
and flush out
toxins;
Which I took willingly and woefully.

It'd do no good, the Lord only knows
how upset everyone would get
Finding out a girl like me,
with a good head on her shoulders
Thinks those dirty thoughts.
Better to be left unheard,
better to be left unread.

So, I'll just stay silent.
I'll have a taste of the pain,
Reflect and appreciate the rain
cleanse myself of the dirty thoughts of today
wash out the worries of just one more bad day.

Vanessa Zimmerman

TASTE AVERSION

You've never gone apple picking. You've never had that sweet juicy freshness, that crunch of an apple taken right from the branch. Never walked down the lanes of the different kinds: deep dark reds to smiling yellows. You've never climbed to the top of a tree fingers just brushing the sour granny smith—slightly out of reach." And I ask you this, ask why someone like you living in Upstate New York has never been. You reply with I don't know, and I leave it be.

My mouth waters at the thought of Apple Fest. in Ithaca. You join me every year, but I guess this is the first time I noticed you spend more time at the Mac-N-Cheese trunk and the fried dough, than any sort of apple infused treat at the festival. I gorge, with ice cream, and donuts, and pizza all apple based. I wide-eyed at the many delicious ways to spend my day always an apple in hand. You, you try the wine, and maple-syrup popcorn. And this time I don't leave it be, like somehow by not eating apples at a festival for apples that her life was one of blasphemy.

And I wish I never did it, asked her a question direct enough not to answer. But I did, in some sarcastic entitled manner I handed her an apple and said, "What are you triggered or something, it's just an apple and it's so good. You need to try it, and I am not taking no for an answer."

And so, she did, ate the apple, said it tasted fresh and crisp and sweet.

I imagine her holding the small bits in her esophagus, a mother bird carrying food half chewed to her nest. I imagine her purging the fruit into her garbage as soon as I dropped her off. I imagine her brushing her teeth, and washing it down with some pumpkin spiced latte.

    It takes 2 years of this cycle, until you finally tell me over candlelight, tea and feelings. How it felt to be taken away, driven to some trailer sunken deep within an apple orchard. How the smell of this migrant worker's hands reminded you of your grandmother's homemade apple pie. His friend's laughter in the other room as rich as the cider. His Adam's apple churning his saliva of burnt caramel. How you finally were released, staggering your way out over fallen, rotting apples. How he didn't take no for an answer.

    You in all your bravery soothe my guilt, you in stoic simplicity remind me that you don't need a festival of apples.
    You tell me that for the past two years, every single day is like walking through an apple orchard and by now there is nothing left to see—or taste.

www.ingramcontent.com/pod-product-compliance
Lightning Source LLC
Chambersburg PA
CBHW071228090426
42736CB00014B/3005